Palm Trees

by Marcia S. Freeman

Consulting Editor:
Gail Saunders-Smith, Ph.D.

Consultant:
Jeff Gillman, Associate Professor
of Nursery Management,
University of Minnesota

Pebble Books

an imprint of Capstone Press
Mankato, Minnesota

Pebble Books are published by Capstone Press
151 Good Counsel Drive, P.O. Box 669, Mankato, Minnesota 56002
http://www.capstone-press.com

2 3 4 5 6 7 07 06 05 04 03

Library of Congress Cataloging-in-Publication Data
Freeman, Marcia S., 1937–
    Palm trees / by Marcia S. Freeman.
    p. cm.—(Trees)
    Summary: Photographs and simple text depict the trunks, leaves, and fruit of
palm trees.
    ISBN 0-7368-0094-8 (hardcover)
    ISBN 0-7368-8095-X (paperback)
    1. Palms—Juvenile literature. [1. Palms. 2. Trees.] I. Title. II. Series.
QK495.P17F74 1999
584'.5—dc21   98-7181

Note to Parents and Teachers

The Trees series supports national science standards for units on
the diversity and unity of plant life. This book describes and
illustrates the parts of palm trees. The photographs support early
readers in understanding the text. The repetition of words and
phrases helps early readers learn new words. This book also
introduces early readers to subject-specific vocabulary words, which
are defined in the Words to Know section. Early readers may need
assistance to read some words and to use the Table of Contents,
Words to Know, Read More, Internet Sites, and Index/Word List
sections of the book.

Table of Contents

Palm trees are tall trees.
They have no branches.

A palm tree has a straight trunk. The trunk is about the same width at the top and the bottom.

A palm tree has smooth or rough bark. Some palm trees have thorns.

Palm fronds grow from the top of a trunk. A frond is a group of leaves.

Some fronds have long stems. Leaves grow on each side of a long stem.

14

Some fronds have short stems. Leaves grow from the end of a short stem.

A palm tree grows flowers. Some flowers make fruit such as dates and coconuts.

Palm seeds grow inside fruit. New palm trees grow from some seeds.

You can tell a palm tree by its trunk and fronds.

Words to Know

coconut—a fruit with a hard, hairy shell; coconuts grow on palm trees and hold seeds.

date—a sticky, brown fruit; dates grow on palm trees and hold palm seeds.

frond—a large, divided leaf on a palm tree

fruit—the fleshy product of a plant; flowers make fruit.

rough—having bumps and dents

smooth—being even and flat

stem—the long main part of a plant from which leaves and flowers grow

straight—not bent or curved

thorn—a sharp point on a branch or a stem of a plant

trunk—the main stem of a tree

width—the distance from one side of something to the opposite side

Read More

Chambers, Catherine. *Bark.* Would You Believe It! Austin, Texas: Raintree Steck-Vaughn, 1996.

Greenaway, Theresa. *Trees.* Pockets. New York: Dorling Kindersley, 1995.

Morgan, Sally. *Flowers, Trees, and Fruits.* Young Discoverers. New York: Kingfisher, 1996.

Internet Sites

Do you want to find out more about palm trees? Let FactHound, our fact-finding hound dog, do the research for you.

Here's how:

1) Visit *http://www.facthound.com*

2) Type in the **Book ID** number: **0736800948**

3) Click on **FETCH IT**.

FactHound will fetch Internet sites picked by our editors just for you!

23

Index/Word List

Word Count: 123
Early-Intervention Level: 13

Editorial Credits

Martha E. Hillman, editor; Clay Schotzko/Icon Productions, cover designer; Sheri Gosewisch, photo researcher

Photo Credits

Betty Crowell, 6
Cheryl R. Richter, cover
Dembinsky Photo Agency/M. Kazmers, 1; John Mielcarek, 12; Mark J. Thomas, 18; Bill Lea, 20
KAC Productions/Kathy Adams Clark, 10
Mark Turner, 14
Rainbow/Jeff Greenberg, 4
Rob Miracle, 8
Unicorn Stock Photos/Mike Morris, 16